D0605312

BLAZERS

EPIC
SPORTS
RECORDS

AMAZING HOCKEY RECORDS

RECORDS

BY THOM STORDEN

WITHDRAWN

Reading Consultant:
Barbara J. Fox
Professor Emerita
North Carolina State University

CAPSTONE PRESS
a capstone imprint

Blazers Books are published by Capstone Press,
1710 Roe Crest Drive, North Mankato, Minnesota 56003
www.capstonepub.com

Library of Congress Cataloging-in-Publication Data
Amazing hockey records / by Thom Storden.
pages cm.—(Blazers Books. Epic sports records.)
Includes bibliographical references and index.
Summary: "Provides information on the most stunning records in the sport of
professional hockey"—Provided by publisher.
Audience: Age: 8-14.
Audience: Grade: 4 to 6.
ISBN 978-1-4914-0742-4 (library binding)
ISBN 978-1-4914-0747-9 (eBook PDF)
1. Hockey—Records—Juvenile literature. I. Title.
GV847.5.S76 2015
796.962—dc23

                        2014008653

Editorial Credits
Nate LeBoutillier, editor; Kyle Grenz, designer; Eric Gohl, media researcher;
Kathy McColley, production specialist

Photo Credits
Dreamstime: Jerry Coli, cover (all); Getty Images: B Bennett, 7, Bruce Bennett
Studios, 20, 26, Focus On Sport, 9, NY Daily News Archive/Charles Hoff,
25, Robert Laberge, 23; Newscom: Icon SMI/IHA, 14, 18, 29, Icon SMI/John
McDonough, 4, NHLI/Denis Brodeur, 13, ZUMA Press/Dick Darrell, 10;
Shutterstock: B Calkins, 1, Shooter Bob Square Lenses, 2–3, 30–31, 32; Wikipedia:
slgckgc, 17

Design Elements: Shuttestock

Records in this book are current through the 2013–14 season.

Printed in the United States of America in Stevens Point, Wisconsin.
122014   008671R

TABLE OF CONTENTS

WAYNE GRETZKY

EPIC//FACT

Wayne Gretzky holds more records
than any other hockey player.

HOW DO WE MEASURE AMAZING?

Hockey is a very **competitive** sport. How do we separate the best from the rest? How do we give credit to incredible performances? How do we make glorious moments in time into golden memories? Keeping records is one way to do it.

competitive—trying to be the best

3 GOALS IN 21 SECONDS

Have you ever seen lightning strike?
On March 23, 1952, the New York Rangers could
have sworn they did. The Chicago Blackhawks
trailed the Rangers, 6–2. Then Blackhawks skater
Bill Mosienko scored 3 goals in 21 seconds.
The Blackhawks used the jolt to win the game.

OTHER SINGLE-GAME SKATER RECORDS

Most Points

10	Darryl **Sittler**, Toronto Maple Leafs February 7, 1976

Most Goals

7	Joe **Malone**, Quebec Bulldogs January 31, 1920

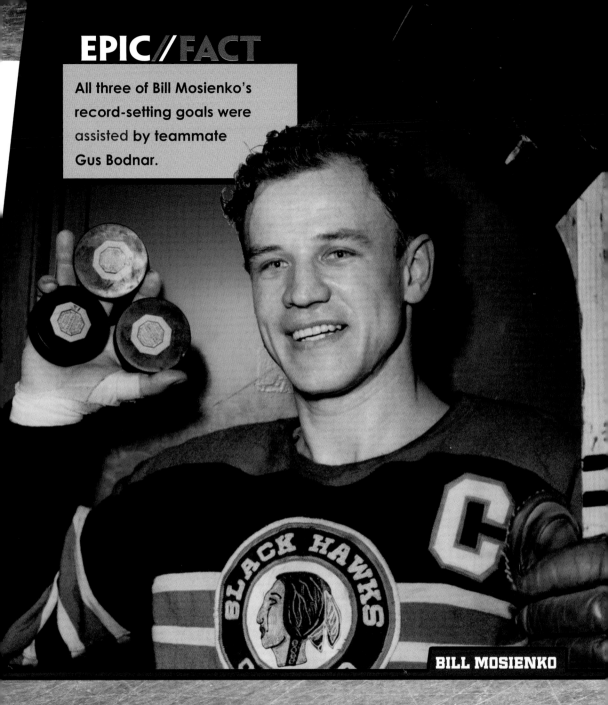

EPIC//FACT

All three of Bill Mosienko's record-setting goals were assisted by teammate Gus Bodnar.

BILL MOSIENKO

MOST POINTS IN A SEASON 215

One of Wayne Gretzky's most amazing records is for scoring 215 **points** in a single season. In 1985–86 he scored 52 goals and passed for 163 assists. Gretzky topped 200 points three other seasons. No other player has ever reached 200.

OTHER SINGLE-SEASON SKATER RECORDS

Most Goals Scored

92 Wayne **Gretzky**
Edmonton Oilers, 1981–82

Most Assists

163 Wayne **Gretzky**
Edmonton Oilers, 1985–86

EPIC//FACT

The most hat tricks in a season is 10.
Wayne Gretzky did this twice.

WAYNE
GRETZKY

points—in hockey, players' points are
calculated by adding up goals and assists

hat trick—a feat achieved when a player
scores three goals in a single game

EPIC//FACT

Gordie Howe played alongside his sons Marty and Mark. The trio played together for seven years for the Houston Aeros and then the Hartford Whalers.

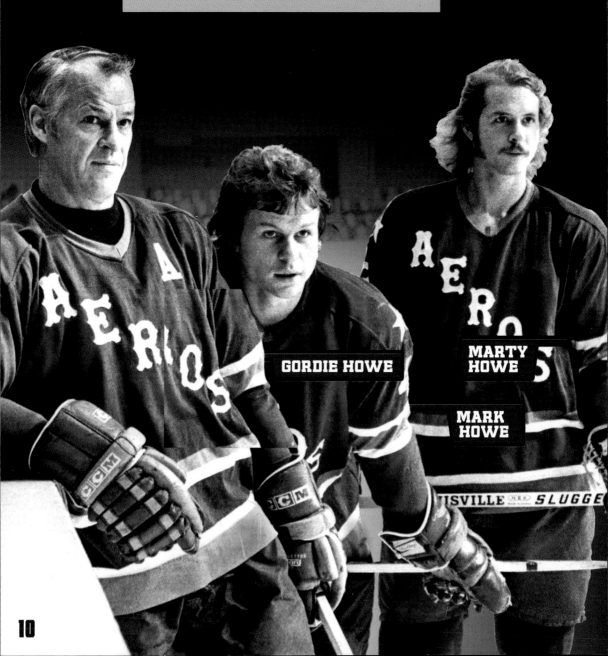

GORDIE HOWE

MARTY HOWE

MARK HOWE

MOST GAMES PLAYED IN A CAREER
1,767

Not many hockey players had a better career than Gordie Howe. No one ever played more games than him—1,767 to be exact. Howe was the oldest player to ever take the ice. In 1980 he played his final pro game at the age of 52.

OTHER INDIVIDUAL RECORDS

Most Hat Tricks
50 Wayne **Gretzky**, four teams

Most Game-Winning Goals
124 Jaromir **Jagr**, seven teams

GOALS IN A SEASON BY A ROOKIE 76

The Winnipeg Jets **drafted** Teemu Selanne when he was just 18 years old. Selanne grew up in Finland and was not ready to make the move. Finally Selanne joined the Jets in 1992 at age 22. Selanne set the record for goals by a **rookie** with 76.

OTHER ROOKIE SKATER RECORDS

Most Assists in a Season

70	Peter **Stastny** Quebec Nordiques, 1980–81 Joe **Juneau** Boston Bruins, 1992–93

Most Shutouts in a Season

15	Tony **Esposito** Chicago Blackhawks, 1969–70

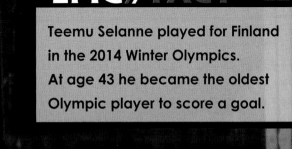

Teemu Selanne played for Finland in the 2014 Winter Olympics. At age 43 he became the oldest Olympic player to score a goal.

TEEMU SELANNE

draft—to choose a new player for a professional team

rookie—a first-year player

13

Bobby Orr led the entire league in points twice while playing with the Boston Bruins.

BOBBY ORR

MOST POINTS BY A DEFENSEMAN IN A SINGLE SEASON 139

Bobby Orr was a **defenseman**. The main part of his job was keeping opponents from scoring. But Orr was also good at scoring and assisting on goals. In the 1970–71 season, he scored 139 points. It was a record for defensemen.

OTHER SINGLE-SEASON GOALIE AND DEFENSEMAN RECORDS

Most Goals by a Defenseman

48 Paul **Coffey**
Edmonton Oilers, 1985–86

Most Wins by a Goalie

48 Martin **Brodeur**
New Jersey Devils, 2006–07

defenseman—a player who tries to stop the other team from scoring

15

MOST TIMES LED THE LEAGUE IN WINS 9

Martin Brodeur has led the National Hockey League (NHL) in wins nine different seasons, a record. He also holds goalie records for games played, **saves**, and total wins. Brodeur won three Stanley Cup championships with the New Jersey Devils.

OTHER CAREER GOALIE AND DEFENSEMAN RECORDS

Most Goals by a Defenseman

395	Ray **Bourque** Boston Bruins, Colorado Avalanche

Most Games Played by a Goalie

1,259	Martin **Brodeur** New Jersey Devils

save—to stop a puck from going into a goal

EPIC//FACT

Martin Brodeur recorded seven shutouts in the 2003 playoffs, an NHL record.

MARTIN BRODEUR

shutout—stopping the opposing team from scoring any points

17

EPIC//FACT

Patrick Roy won the Stanley Cup twice with the Montreal Canadiens. He also won it twice with the Colorado Avalanche.

PATRICK ROY

MOST POSTSEASON CAREER WINS BY A GOALIE 151

Patrick Roy played goalie in the NHL for 18 full seasons. His teams made the playoffs in 17 of those seasons. As a result, Roy won 151 playoff games in goal, the most ever. Only one other goalie, Martin Brodeur, has topped 100 postseason wins.

OTHER CAREER POSTSEASON RECORDS

Most Career Goals

122 Wayne **Gretzky**, four teams

Most Career Assists

260 Wayne **Gretzky**, four teams

Jean Beliveau scored a game-winning goal in the Stanley Cup Finals nine times.

JEAN BELIVEAU

MOST CAREER POINTS IN THE STANLEY CUP FINALS 62

Jean Beliveau played for the Montreal Canadiens. The Canadiens were a very good team. Beliveau played his best when the Canadiens were in the Stanley Cup Finals. Beliveau played in the NHL's championship 13 times and scored a record 62 points.

OTHER CAREER STANLEY CUP FINALS RECORDS

Most Goals in Stanley Cup Finals

34	Maurice **Richard** Montreal Canadiens

Most Assists in Stanley Cup Finals

35	Wayne **Gretzky** Edmonton Oilers

MOST CHAMPIONSHIPS WON BY A FRANCHISE 23

The Stanley Cup was first awarded in 1892. Lord Frederick Stanley, the Governor General of Canada, offered it to the best hockey team in Canada. The National Hockey League took over the trophy in 1910. Since then the Montreal Canadiens have won it 23 times.

Most Stanley Cups, Franchise

23	Montreal **Canadiens**
13	Toronto **Maple Leafs**
11	Detroit **Red Wings**

franchise—a professional sports team

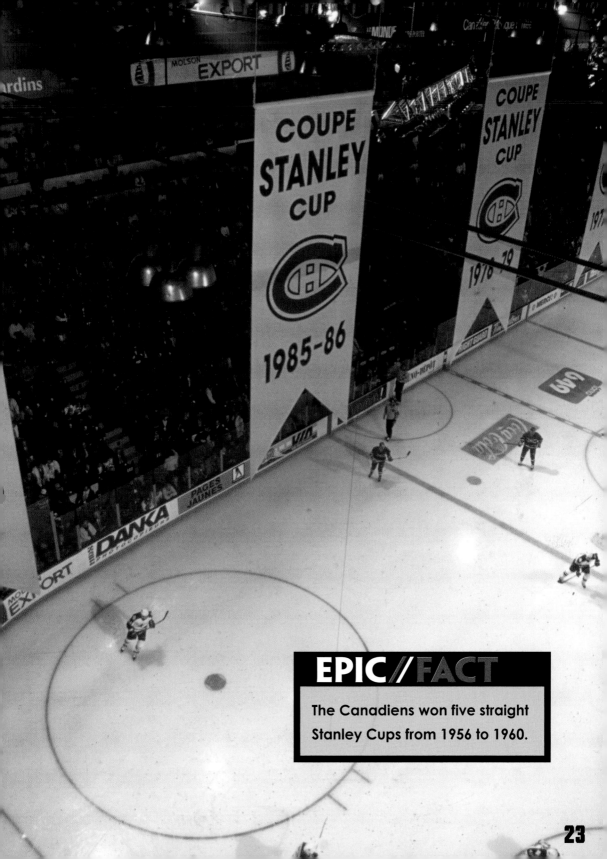

EPIC//FACT

The Canadiens won five straight Stanley Cups from 1956 to 1960.

MOST STANLEY CUPS WON BY AN INDIVIDUAL 11

Henri Richard is the one and only player to win 11 Stanley Cups. Henri was the younger brother and Montreal Canadiens teammate of Maurice Richard, one of hockey's all-time **legends**. Maurice often led the Canadiens in goals. Henri often led the club in assists.

OTHER FAMOUS FIRSTS RECORDS

First Woman to Appear in NHL Competition

Manon **Rheaume**, Tampa Bay Lightning, 1992

First to Score 50 Goals in 50 Games

Maurice **Richard**, Montreal Canadiens, 1945

Henri Richard was 15 years younger than his brother, Maurice. They were teammates in Montreal for five years.

MAURICE RICHARD

HENRI RICHARD

legend—one of the all-time greats; known for amazing feats

CHRIS NILAN

MOST PENALTIES IN ONE GAME BY A SINGLE PLAYER 10

Chris Nilan spent 42 minutes in the penalty box on March 31, 1991. That night he set the record for most penalties in a game with 10. Nilan's nickname was "Knuckles" because he loved to fight.

OTHER EMBARRASSING RECORDS

Most Penalty Minutes, Season

472 Dave **Schultz**, Philadelphia Flyers, 1974–75

Most Penalty Minutes, Career

3,966 Tiger **Williams**, five teams

MOST CONSECUTIVE GAMES IN GOAL 502

From 1955 to 1962, hockey fans could count on Glen Hall, known as "Mr. Goalie." Hall played 502 straight regular season games in goal. The number of games he played in a row is actually 551 if you count playoff games. The streak lasted more than seven years.

OTHER RECORD STREAKS

Longest Win Streak

17	Pittsburgh Penguins 1992–93

Glen Hall played goalie without a mask. He received some 250 stitches in his face during his career.

GLEN HALL

GLOSSARY

assist (ah-SIST)—a pass that leads to a score

competitive (kum-PET-i-tiv)—very eager to be the best

defenseman (de-FENS-mun)—a player who tries to stop the other team from scoring

draft (DRAFT)—to choose a new player for a professional team

franchise (FRAN-chize)—professional sports team

hat trick (HAT TRIK)—a feat achieved when a player scores three goals in a single game

legend (LEJ-und)—one of the all-time greats, known for amazing feats

points (POINTS)—in hockey, players' points are ccalculated by adding up goals and assists

postseason (POST-see-sun)—the playoffs following the regular season where teams battle for the championship

rookie (RUHK-ee)—a first-year player

save (SAYV)—to stop a puck from going into a goal

shutout (SHUT-out)—stopping the opposing team from scoring any points

READ MORE

Frederick, Shane *The Best of Everything Hockey Book.* North Mankato, Minn.: Capstone Press. 2011.

Sports Illustrated Kids STATS!: The Greatest Numbers in Sports. New York: Time Home Entertainment, Inc., 2013.

INTERNET SITES

FactHound offers a safe, fun way to find Internet sites related to this book. All of the sites on FactHound have been researched by our staff.

Here's all you do:

Visit *www.facthound.com*

Type in this code: 9781491407424

Super-cool stuff! Check out projects, games and lots more at www.capstonekids.com

INDEX